PAPER
The Brown Bag
MAKING
Paper Art
BOOK

A COLLECTION OF PAPERMAKING TECHNIQUES,
IDEAS AND PROJECTS FOR USE WITH BROWN BAG PAPER ART™
AND BROWN BAG COOKIE ART® CERAMIC MOLDS

by Lucy Ross Natkiel
Photography by Bruce Cramer

© 1995 Hill Design, Inc.
Concord, New Hampshire 03301

Table of Contents

Introduction

I suppose our love affair with handmade paper had a round-about beginning.

In 1983, we started making Brown Bag Cookie Art ceramic cookie molds. These molds made it possible to really play with cookie baking in a way that had never been possible. As time passed, we developed more and more ways to enjoy the molds. First, we expanded the baking possibilities with lots of new cookie recipes. Then came two-tone cookies and ice cream sandwiches made with molded cookies. Using the molds to form fanciful chocolates followed, and the *Gourmet Cookie Book* came into being.

But we weren't the only ones who were experimenting and playing with our molds. Soon we began getting letters from customers with examples of all the wonderful projects they had made with the molds. There were fragrant cinnamon pomanders, beautifully painted baker's clay and beeswax ornaments, "stained glass" cookies and more. We wrote the *Brown Bag Idea Book* to share all the ideas.

Then came paper casting. It was a revelation. We found how easy it was to make spectacular bas relief paper castings using our molds and very basic paper making technology.

A whole new world of possibilities opened up. And as with the cookie molds, the more we explored this new world, the more exciting it became. Ideas started flowing for even more ways to use molds with paper. How about molds for three-dimensional images or fold-up ornaments? What about really delicate relief work? Color? Glitter? Fancy decorations? We wondered what all could be done - then we got busy. Brown Bag Paper Art, a whole new range of products with all its specialty molds and supplies, is the outcome of all this excitement.

In this book we provide a lot of basic information on paper making techniques, from flat sheets to molded three- dimensional forms, as well as interesting uses of molds, painting techniques, ideas for wonderful projects and more. Most of the projects utilize Brown Bag Cookie Art and Brown Bag Paper Art ceramic molds.

Best of all, here is an introduction to some of the possibilities afforded by a fascinating craft. You'll quickly discover that the field is limitless. Let your imagination and creativity run wild. Have fun! We hope you will become as excited as we are with making your own handcast paper.

A Short History of Papermaking

Paper is made of the bonded fibers of various plant materials. Wood, cotton, flax, rice straw and certain other grasses are beaten to expose the cellulose, then mixed with water to form a slurry. This mixture is run through a sieve, and the fibrous material remaining is dried in a mold to form paper. Essentially, papermaking is a felting process.

Long ago, before the invention of paper, people wrote on thin strips of wood, scrolls of woven cloth, on parchment, vellum or papyrus. Though these served the same function, none was a true paper. (Parchment and vellum are made from split and stretched animal skins, and papyrus is made of the laminated pith of a river grass, of the same name.) They were expensive and unavailable except to the elite.

About two thousand years ago in China, a man named Ts'ai Lun made the first real hand-made paper. The first sheets were quite rough, but papermaking techniques soon improved, and paper became the most popular and widely available writing surface. The knowledge about how to make paper was a closely guarded secret in China for 500 years.

But knowledge has a way of spreading. Early in the 7th century A.D., papermaking made its way into Korea, then Japan. In the 8th century, the knowledge migrated to the Middle East, and from there, west.

A thousand years after Ts'ai Lun's discovery, paper making was introduced into Europe. Most of the subsequent European papers were made from cotton and linen.

In 1719, a French naturalist by the name of René de Reaumur was intrigued by wasps building their paper-like nests of chewed wood. He tried using wood pulp to make paper and found that this worked very well. Most of the paper we now use every day is made from wood pulp, though fine writing and drawing papers are still made from cotton and linen fibers, just as they have been for a thousand years.

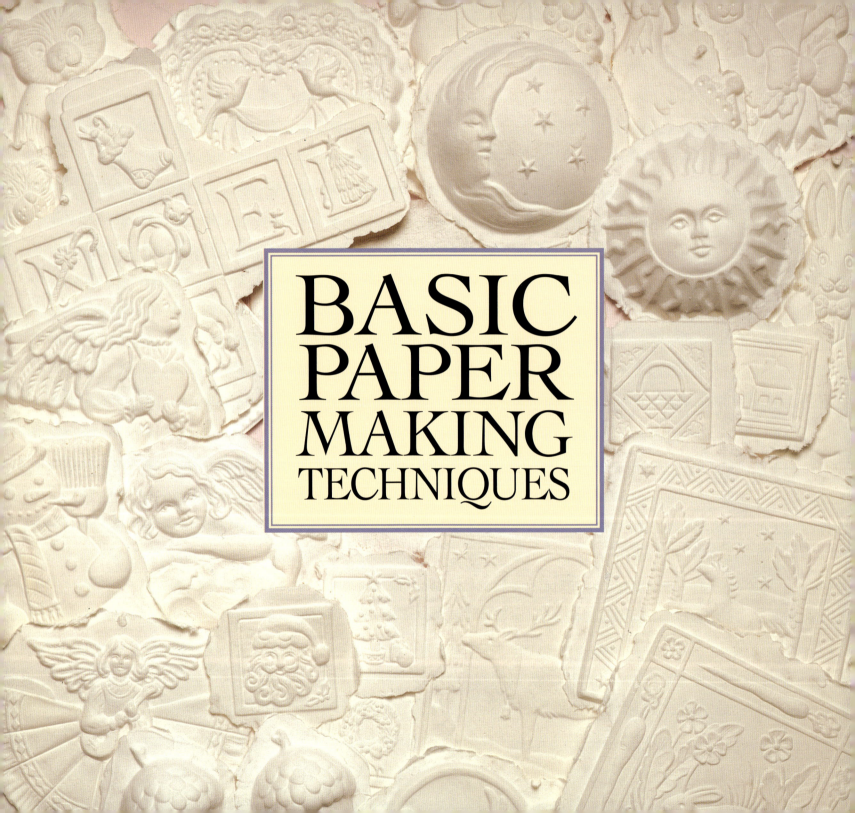

BASIC
PAPER
MAKING
TECHNIQUES

Making Paper Pulp

Though you can make paper from a number of different fibers, all the paper projects in this book are made using a pulp made from pure cotton linter - a heavy cardboard-like material made from roughly compressed cotton fibers. It is almost a thick, unrefined paper, and it is used extensively in the manufacture of durable, high quality cotton papers. Paper money is made principally from cotton linter.

Here is how to go about making paper pulp from cotton linter:

You will need:

cotton linter sheets
"Paper Clay", an additive that improves fiber to fiber
  bonding and increases the hardness of the paper's
  surface. This is not absolutely necessary, but it helps.
kitchen blender
sieve
sponge
kitchen towels

Dip a 7" x 8" sheet of cotton linter into cold water then tear into small pieces, about 2" square.

Place the torn linter in the jar of a Kitchen Blender along with 1 quart of cold water and allow it to soak and soften for at least 10 minutes.

Blend the water and the linter at slow speed for 1 minute. Add 1 teaspoon of "Paper Clay" and increase the speed to high. Blend for 20 seconds, pause for 10 seconds, blend again for 20 seconds. You now have paper pulp.

Note: Be careful not to put undue strain on your blender. Be sure you have plenty of water in your mix, and always have "resting periods" to allow the motor to cool down. Stop the blender immediately if it seems to be laboring, and remove some of the pulp.

Wet pulp can be stored for a couple of weeks in a sealed container. If the pulp acquires an odor, mix in 1/2 teaspoon of bleach per quart of material. Rinse the pulp well in a strainer before you use it.

Left over pulp can also be dried for later use. Pour the pulp into a sieve, then gather it into a ball and squeeze out as much water as you can. Set the ball aside to dry. When you want to reconstitute it, break off a piece, and soak it in water to soften before whizzing it in the blender. You will not need to add more "Paper Clay" to reconstituted pulp.

Casting Paper in Flat Molds

Use these instructions to cast paper pulp in Brown Bag Cookie Art molds and the flat Brown Bag Paper Art molds. The Three-Dimensional Paper Art molds require a slightly different technique.

2

3

1. Make a batch of paper pulp, as described on the previous page.

2. Pour about 1 cup of paper pulp from the blender into a sieve to drain slightly. It should still be very wet. Pour the pulp into your mold, set on a folded kitchen towel.

3. Spread the pulp evenly over the mold, making sure that you cover the edges as well. The uneven edges around the border of your paper casting will add a delicate, "hand-made" touch. The pulp should cover the surface of the mold thinly and evenly.

4. Gently press the paper pulp into the mold with a sponge. Wring out and repeat.

5. Using a folded kitchen towel, press the pulp firmly into the mold. This will absorb more water, and will insure that the paper picks up all the detail from the mold. It is important to press out as much water as possible. Excess water left in the pulp will produce a paper casting with a wrinkled finish.

6. Dry the pulp *completely* in the mold by leaving it on the counter overnight to dry, in the sun for 4 hours, or in a 150° oven for 3 hours. You can also dry it in the microwave. Place your pulp filled mold in the center of the microwave oven and set on full power for 1 minute. Rotate the mold 1/2 turn, and microwave for another 30 seconds. Continue until the paper is completely dry. *Note: Molds dried in a microwave can be hot. Be careful not to burn yourself.*

7. When the paper is *completely dry,* carefully lift the edges with a small sharp knife and peel the paper out of the mold. Scrub the mold with hot, soapy water and a vegetable brush to clean and to prevent fiber build up that might result in sticking in future castings. If fiber build up does occur, however, boil the mold for 10 minutes, and allow it to cool.

Your castings should be thin. If not, you'll get fewer images from a sheet of cotton linter, and they'll be heavy. If for any reason you want to redo your casting, simply put it back in the blender with some water and start again. You won't have to add more "Paper Clay."

4

5

7

9

Three-Dimensional Casting

These instructions work for papercastings in deep molds, whether a Brown Bag Paper Art Three-Dimensional mold, or a beautiful, deep shell that you find on the beach.

2

4

1. Make a batch of paper pulp, as described on page 7.

2. Pour the contents of your blender into a sieve to drain until the water stops running and just drips. Set the pulp filled sieve in a bowl just large enough to hold it. The pulp will be very wet.

3. Rinse the inside of your mold with cool water and place on a folded kitchen towel.

4. If you are using one of the Brown Bag Paper Art 3-D molds that has two casting images, take large pinches of pulp and build up a *thin, even layer* in one cavity. (The pulp will be dripping wet). Make sure the pulp extends as far as the guide lines around the border of the cavity. This ragged border will add a delicate, "hand-made" touch.

If you are casting paper into a shell or some other such object, proceed in the same manner, except you won't have a border around the image. Instead, be sure to make the pulp a little thicker at the edge of your casting, and make the edge as even as possible. You will probably want to trim the edge with scissors when the casting is dry.

5. Gently press the pulp into the mold with a sponge. Wring out the sponge and repeat. The pressure of the sponge may pull the pulp away from the edge of the mold. To correct this, take a small amount of pulp from the sieve and patch. It is important to patch all holes and thin spots before you proceed further. If you are using a mold with two images, repeat steps 4 & 5 with the second cavity of the mold.

6. Using a folded kitchen towel, press the pulp firmly into the mold. This will absorb more water, and will insure that the paper picks up all

the detail from the mold. When you finish with one image, do the other. It is important to press out as much water as possible. Excess water left in the pulp will produce a paper casting with a wrinkled finish.

If you are casting paper in a shell, cradle it in one hand while you firmly press the towel into it to absorb water. Shells are fragile, and if you press down on one while it is lying on a hard counter, it might break.

5

7. *Dry the pulp completely in the mold* by leaving it on the counter overnight to dry, in the sun for 4 hours, or in a 150° oven for 3 hours. You can also dry it in the microwave. Place your pulp filled mold in the center of the microwave oven and set on full power for 1 minute. Rotate the mold 1/2 turn, and microwave for another 30 seconds. Continue until the paper is completely dry. *Note: Molds dried in a microwave can be hot. Be careful not to burn yourself.* Do not try to speed dry paper cast in a natural shell in the microwave.

6

8. When the paper is *completely dry,* carefully lift the edges with a small, sharp knife and peel the paper out of the mold. Scrub the mold with hot, soapy water and a vegetable brush to clean and prevent fiber build up that might result in sticking in future castings. If fiber build up does occur, however, boil for 10 minutes, and allow to cool.

Your castings should be thin. If not, you'll get fewer images from a sheet of cotton linter, and they'll be heavy. If for any reason you want to redo your casting, simply put it back in the blender with some water and start again. You won't have to add more "Paper Clay."

8

For extra easy removal of 3-D paper castings, lightly spray your mold with Silicone before you begin. Allow the Silicone to dry before using the mold. Five or six castings can be made before you need to respray. Don't wash your mold between castings if you have sprayed it with Silicone. If you are planning to use your mold for food later on, don't spray it.

Making Sheets of Paper

Handmade sheets of paper have a character that cannot be duplicated by a commercial paper mill. They are beautiful in and of themselves, make unique writing papers, and can be used as interesting backgrounds for your paper castings.

These are simplified instructions for making fairly small sheets of paper. If you are interested in making a lot of large sheets, check the information in one of the books listed in the Bibliography. They cover a number of more sophisticated couching, pressing and drying techniques.

You will need:

paper pulp (see page 7)
sponge
kitchen towels
papermaking frame and deckle (see appendix)
large rubber bands
plastic tub, larger than your papermaking frame
nylon window screen, a few inches larger than your
 papermaking frame
blotter made of white felt, larger than the sheets of
 paper you intend to make. Felt made of natural
 fibers absorb water better than synthetics.

1. Fill your plastic tub half way with water.

2. Place the empty frame, or deckle, on top of the papermaking frame so that the screening of the paper frame is sandwiched in the middle. Place rubber bands around the frames to hold them together. Float this prepared paper sheet mold in the tub of water, deckle side up.

2

4

3. Make a batch of paper pulp.

4. Pour about 1 to 1 1/2 cups of paper pulp into the floating paper mold. Pat the pulp lightly with your finger tips to spread it evenly in the mold. Add a little more pulp to fill gaps, or take out a little if the pulp looks too thick. It should be quite thin, but the pulp should cover the area completely. You'll soon develop a feel for what's right.

5. Holding the frame level, lift it out of the tub, and let the water drain for about 20 seconds. Tip the sheet mold, and let it drain for another 10 seconds.

6. Remove the rubber bands and lift off the deckle. Place the piece of nylon screening over the newly formed sheet of paper, and press it gently with the sponge. Peel up the nylon screen.

7. Fold a kitchen towel in half, and place it on the counter to form a thin pad. Be sure there are no wrinkles. Turn the paper frame over onto the towel. With another towel, press firmly on the piece of paper through the screening.

5

6

7

8

9

10

8. Slowly lift the frame off the paper.

9. Turn the towel over onto a felt blotter. Slowly peel the towel off the paper.

Flatten your paper by alternating layers of felt and handmade paper, then placing several heavy books on top for a day or two.

10. If you want to use your handmade paper right away, dry and press it flat with an electric iron. Just place the sheet of damp paper between two dry kitchen towels. Turn your iron onto medium hot, or the "wool" setting, and press the paper through the towels. Press one side until it feels quite dry, then turn over and press the other side.

Variations:

Once you have mastered making a sheet of plain paper, you can start to play with variations. Add bits of colored or metallic threads, glitter, grasses, petals, or tiny leaves and flowers to the pulp in the blender. If you try this, add only a small amount during the final 5 seconds of blending. The paper looks nicer when the grasses or flowers act as an accent. You might want to tint your paper. (See "Coloring The Paper Pulp", page 26.)

Laminating

When making sheets of paper, you can achieve a number of interesting effects by laminating handmade papers of different colors and textures. It is easy to do.

You will need:
two batches of paper pulp of differing colors.
all of the materials listed under Making Sheets of Paper (page 12)
additional piece of nylon screening

1. Make a very thin sheet of paper from one of the batches of paper pulp, using the method described in the section on "Making Sheets of Paper," page 12, but with this difference: when you pour the paper pulp into the frame, pour in about half of what you would ordinarily. As you pat the pulp to distribute it evenly, it won't completely cover the area, and will look too thin. Don't worry. This is as it should be. You might even want to have the pulp cover only part of the open area in the frame.

2. Lift the frame from the tub and allow it to drain.

Remove the deckle. Place the piece of nylon screening over the newly formed sheet of paper and press it with a sponge.

3. Now, holding the screening in place over the paper, flip the whole frame over onto a folded kitchen towel. With a dry towel, pat the paper through the screen of the paper frame. Carefully lift the frame off of the paper, leaving it on the piece of nylon screening.

4. Make another sheet of paper from the second batch of paper pulp, but this time make it a normal thickness. Remove the sheet from the mold and lay it on a folded towel, as usual.

5. Pick up the piece of nylon screening with the first, thin sheet of paper still adhering to it, and flip the screening over onto your second, thicker piece of paper.

6. Press through the screening with a sponge. Press again with a dry dish towel. Starting at one corner, peel the screening off the paper.

7. Place a felt over the laminated paper and weight it for 24 hours. Remove the felt and the weight, and allow the paper to dry completely.

Embedding

There are some perfectly beautiful handmade Japanese papers that have leaves and butterfly wings layered in the paper. Though embedding different accent materials really isn't suitable for handcast paper made in molds, it is a wonderful treatment for sheets of paper, and for projects made using the decorated sheets. A gift box with a dried, pressed pansy embedded in the box top is a truly unique and special present all by itself. (See the instructions on page 66 for making gift boxes from your own sheets of paper.)

Here are instructions for embedding small, flat accent materials in a sheet of paper.

You will need:
*all of the materials listed under
   "Making Sheets of Paper" (page 12)
batch of paper pulp, tinted or untinted
dried, pressed materials to laminate
   (flowers, leaves, etc.)*

1. Fill your plastic tub half way with water.

2. Assemble the frame and deckle as described on page 12. Float the prepared paper sheet mold in the tub of water, deckle side up.

3. Pour about 1 to 1-1/2 cups of paper pulp into the floating paper mold. Pat the pulp lightly with your finger tips to spread it evenly in the mold.

4. Take the dried, pressed accent materials that you want to embed, and position them on top of the paper pulp in the floating mold. As you put each item on the pulp, press down gently, wiggling your finger as you do so. Float a little bit of the pulp over the top of whatever you are embedding. These fibers will hold the accent material in place when the paper dries.

5. Holding the frame level, lift it out of the tub, and let it drain.

6. Lift off the deckle. Place the piece of nylon screening over the decorated sheet of paper, and press it gently with the sponge. Peel up the nylon screen.

7. Remove the sheet of paper to a folded kitchen towel, and proceed as you would with a plain sheet of paper. It usually isn't a good idea to iron dry a sheet of paper that has embedded accent materials in it.

Embossing

Embossed sheets of paper can be subtle and elegant. Essentially what you are doing when you emboss paper is taking a relief print of an object, such as a leaf. The process is very easy.

Take a damp sheet of handmade paper and drape it over whatever you want to imprint in your paper. Flat, heavily textured items usually work best. Pieces of cotton lace, flat sections of baskets, and thick veined leaves are great.

Press the paper firmly onto the object, using a pad made by bunching up a kitchen towel into a ball. The paper fibers will mold around the object. Lay the damp embossed paper on a felt, cover with another felt, and place a weight on top. Leave the paper in place to dry for a couple of days.

Embossing with Cut Linoleum Blocks

You can also make wonderful embossed paper using a cut linoleum block rather than found objects.

You will need:
linoleum block (available at art supply stores)
linoleum knife set (available at art supply stores)
soft pencil
kitchen towel
electric iron
damp handmade sheet of paper
felt, the size of your design

1. Draw your design on the block of linoleum, keeping in mind that the final embossed print will be reversed.

2. Cover the block with a damp kitchen towel, and iron it at low temperature. The heat will soften the linoleum and make it easier to cut.

3. Carefully cut out your design. As linoleum knives are sharp, always cut away from yourself.

3

5

4. When you have finished cutting, wash the top of the block with warm soapy water to remove any traces of pencil lead.

5. Drape the damp sheet of handmade paper over the block, and firmly press it into all the grooves with a kitchen towel.

6. Cover the damp paper with a felt and place a weight on top. Leave the paper in place to dry for several days.

7. Remove the weight and peel the paper off the linoleum block. Allow it to air dry completely. Paint and decorate your embossed paper as you choose.

Embossing - String Reliefs

You can glue string to a backing board to make a pattern in relief, all ready to emboss. Here, we have made a playful border for one of our handcast paper images. It makes a charming piece of framed art for a child's room.

You will need:
scissors
cotton string with a hard finish
rubber cement
sturdy cardboard
pencil
damp sheet of handmade paper the size of your design

1. Cut the cardboard to the size you want for the finished piece.

2. Draw your design directly on the cardboard, keeping in mind that the pattern will be reversed in the final art.

3. Working a section at a time, paint a thin coat of rubber cement on your design. Next, cut string into pieces, and coat them with rubber cement. Let the string dry slightly, then apply it to the areas of the design that have been coated with cement. Allow the rubber cement to dry completely.

4. Take a sheet of handmade paper large enough to cover your design. While it is still damp, drape it over the string relief. Press the paper firmly against the string relief using a bunched up kitchen towel. Cover the paper with a dry felt and put a weight on top. Allow the paper to dry overnight.

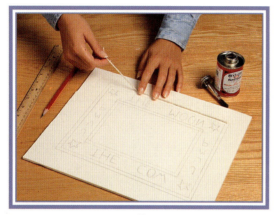

3

4

5. Remove the weight and the felt, and let the paper dry completely.

6. Carefully run a butter knife around the edge of the paper to loosen it, then peel it off of the cardboard backing.

You are now ready to decorate your string relief embossed paper. We have glued a hand-cast paper image to ours, and have added color. *Painting instructions are on pages 27 through 33.*

5

6

Sizing Paper

Hand made paper is quite absorbent. If you want to write on it with calligraphy ink, or if you want a harder, less absorbent surface to paint on, you will have to "size" your paper. Sizing also adds strength to paper.

To size paper that is already dry, dissolve 1 teaspoon of unflavored gelatin in 1 cup of very hot water. While it is still hot, brush or spray the mixture directly on your paper. If you use a spray bottle, be sure you wash it immediately and thoroughly with hot water as soon as you are done, as gelatin will clog the nozzle.

Allow the paper to dry completely before writing or painting on it.

You can also size paper in the pulp stage. To do so, simply add 2 teaspoons of "Paper Clay" to the pulp in the blender, rather than 1 teaspoon. Form the images as usual.

This technique is best used with paper cast in ceramic cookie or paper molds; it is of minimal value if you are making sheets of paper. It doesn't produce a paper with as hard a finish for writing and painting as does the gelatin method, but it is quick and very easy.

DECORATING TECHNIQUES FOR CAST PAPER

*T*hough hand made paper has a beautiful, sometimes ethereal quality all its own, it is hard to resist decorating further. The possibilities for adding color, sparkle, ribbons and flowers seem limitless, and seductive.

In this section, we would like to share what we have learned about various decorating techniques. You can use any of them alone or in conjunction to create very personal works of art.

Coloring the Paper Pulp

You can tint the paper itself by adding color to the water in the blender before you add the cotton linter. Simply add about 2 teaspoons of acrylic paint to 1 quart of tepid water in the jar of a kitchen blender. Whiz to mix. Wet one sheet of 7" x 8" cotton linter and tear it into 2" pieces. Place the torn linter in the colored water and allow to soak for ten minutes. Process and form your paper as usual.

Wash out your blender jar thoroughly, using hot soapy water.

Paper made by this method will be fairly light in color. It is possible to get dark, intense colors, but to do so, you would have to use commercial papermaking pigments and fixatives that are quite toxic. We do not recommend them for home use. Use a dark wash of paint over your paper after it is dry if you want to intensify the color.

You can also tint your paper by adding a torn up sheet of colored construction paper to the cotton linter pulp in the blender jar. You may need to add more water to the mixture.

If you would like your paper to have an antique look, you can color the pulp with very strong tea. Brew a quart of tea, using double the number of tea bags you would normally. Remove the bags and pour the hot tea into the blender jar. Soak a torn up sheet of cotton linter for about an hour, then proceed as usual.

Painting Cast Paper

There are a number of different painting mediums that work well with cast paper. Each has its own advantages and limitations. Choose the one that will best suit your project.

WATERCOLORS

When we were children, many of us were introduced to painting with a box of brightly colored watercolor tablets. I know I loved mine.

Now watercolors come two ways. Brown Bag Paper Art™ sells a boxed set of watercolor tablets designed especially for use with hand-cast papers. These are inexpensive, very easy to use, and don't tend to run or "bleed," the way most tablet and tube watercolors do. Just wet your brush in a clean jar of water, rub it around on the color tablet and paint. You can mix colors in one of the little recessed pockets in the top of the paint box to add breadth to your palette. These watercolors are especially good for children and people who are just getting started painting cast paper.

Watercolors are also available in tubes, and in a myriad of colors. I think there are six different shades of blue in the art store I frequent. One of the advantages of tube watercolors is the breath-taking scope of colors available.

If you decide to use tube watercolors, you will first need to set up your palette. A plain, white dinner plate works well. Squeeze small amounts of paint around the perimeter of the plate. I go from black, to brown, to blues, greens, yellows, orange, red, violet and purple. I usually squeeze out two small mounds of white a little distance away from the other colors. You can mix colors in the center area of the plate.

You will also need a jar of clean water. Change it as it gets dirty, so you won't muddy the colors with which you are painting.

Tube watercolors can be used to create two very different effects. If you thin your paints with just a little water, the colors will be intense and opaque. Though cast paper is quite absorbent, thick paint won't tend to run or "bleed".

If you want thin, translucent washes, dilute the paint with a lot of water. You can get pale, subtle effects with washes that cannot be duplicated with any other painting medium. Washes

are, however, a bit hard to control until you get the hang of it.

As you apply washes, use a brush with only a moderate amount of paint on it. Since cast paper will quickly absorb the thin paint, work a little distance away from the edge of the area you want to color. This way, the paper fibers themselves will draw the paint where you want it. Allow one area to dry before you paint the adjacent one.

When you are finished painting, wash your brushes carefully with water and a little bit of mild soap. You need not wash up your palette. When you start painting again, just add a bit of water to the colors and brush them.

TEMPERA PAINTS

These are the paints used in elementary schools. There is a reason; they are very easy to work with. Tempera's only drawback is that the selection of colors is limited. They are, however, clear and intense. They do not bleed when applied to cast paper, unless you thin them with too much water. Tempera is a good choice to use when working with children.

Since tempera is much more fluid than tube watercolors, you will have to set up differently. Go to an art supply store and purchase a white plastic paint tray that has small wells in it. A white plastic ice cube tray will work, too.

Squeeze some paint into each of the wells. Leave a couple of wells empty, in case you want to mix colors in them. The paint should be the consistency of heavy cream. Thin it with water if it seems too thick.

As with watercolors, let one area dry before painting the one next to it.

Rinse your brush in a jar of clean water each time you switch colors. Wash your paint tray and brushes with water and a little mild soap when you are finished using them.

ACRYLICS

Acrylic paints produce intense colors that don't bleed. They are available in a wide range of hues, including iridescent gold. The colors are a bit brighter than watercolors, and they are easier to handle. You can even paint adjacent areas, if you haven't thinned your paint with too much water.

Acrylics come in a fluid, pre-mixed form in jars, and in tubes. The ready mixed jars of acrylic paints are available in many craft and hobby stores, and are less expensive than the tube paints. The range of colors is, however, more limited.

Set up for painting with fluid acrylics exactly as you would with tempera, pouring small amounts of paint into the wells of a plastic paint or ice cube tray. Be sure to wash up thoroughly when you are done, as it is very hard to clean acrylics off surfaces once dry.

Tube acrylics are sold in art supply stores. They are available in an enormous range of colors, and they last a long time. The only draw-back to tube acrylics is the fact that they dry very quickly. It is a good idea to squeeze out only as much paint as you will need right away, rather than laying out a whole palette of colors at once.

The best palette to use with tube acrylic paints are the throw-way paper ones available on pads at art supply stores, or white paper plates. Keep a jar of clean water handy so that you can rinse your brushes thoroughly each time you change colors.

Tube acrylic paint has a thick, almost jelly-like consistency. You will need to thin it to the consistency of heavy cream, using Acrylic Gloss Medium or water. There is also a product made by Winsor & Newton called Acrylic Flow Improver™ that works very well.

There are a number of brands of gold acrylic paint on the market, each with slightly different characteristics. Liquitex makes an "Iridescent Gold" which, though quite transparent and pale itself, mixes beautifully with other acrylic colors to produce a whole range of shimmering hues. For example, if you want to make an Acorn Ornament with a burnished copper cap, mix some Red Iron Oxide with some Iridescent Gold. The effect is stunning.

Be sure to wash out your brushes with soap and water as soon as you are done painting. Pay special attention to the "ferrules," the place where the bristles are joined to the handle with a metal band, as paint seems to collect there.

MARKING PENS

Marking pens produce vivid colors, are clean, neat and easy to use. The markers that have a brush-like tip at one end are best for use with handcast paper.

Markers have several draw-backs, however. The intense colors cannot be mixed, and they lack subtlety. They also tend to bleed slightly, though this is not a problem for most castings, since the bleeding is minimal. Wait until one area is dry before going on to the one adjacent.

Markers are a natural for decorating Handcast Quilt Greeting Cards and Tags. This is one place, however, that the small amount of bleeding can be annoying; you want the fine, straight lines and little triangles to be crisp and neat. The way to accomplish this is to "size" your paper castings with a gelatin solution and let it dry before decorating. (See page 23) Then, there will be no problem at all.

METALLIC PAINTS

There are three main types of water based metallic paints.

Acrylic Metallics

Acrylic metallic paints vary remarkably from manufacturer to manufacturer. Some, such as Liquitex®, are transparent. Others, such as those made by Jo Sonja®, are opaque and intense. You will have to experiment to see what you like best. Acrylic metallic paints can be mixed with other acrylic paints with varying degrees of success. All should be used with other acrylic paints, or on completely dry castings that have been painted with some other medium.

Metallic Enamels

There are little jars of water based metallic enamels on the market that are in a class by themselves. These produce an opulent, opaque gold or silver that is durable and very beautiful. They do not mix with other paints, however, and you cannot paint other colors over them. Use them at the end of whatever project you are working on. They tend to be expensive.

Powdered Metallic Watercolors

Powdered metallic watercolor paints are wonderful and come in an assortment of colors, ranging from Autumn, Egyptian or Lemon Gold through Silver and Copper. They are hard to find at art stores, but can be ordered through the mail. (See *Sources* at the back of this book.)

They mix easily with water, though they tend to rub off and will eventually tarnish. To avoid tarnishing and rub off, mix with Acrylic Gloss Medium for greater durability. (Follow exact instructions which come with the product you purchase.) Mix powdered metallic watercolor paints in with any paint you choose - watercolor, acrylic or tempera.

You can also apply metallic watercolor paints on top of dried watercolor, acrylic or tempera paint. The effect is beautiful. Though you can apply these metallic paints over non-metallic paint, you can't reverse the order; it won't cover. Count on adding touches of gold and silver to your work last.

Wash your brushes with lots of water. The tiny metal particles in the paint tend to stick in the ferrules of your brush and add sparkle to whatever color you use next, whether you want it or not.

Decorating With Glitter

You can further personalize projects made with handcast paper by gluing a variety of materials either to the casting itself, or to the surrounding card or mat board. Here are a few ideas.

GLITTER

Glitter can add snap and sparkle to your paper castings. It can catch and reflect light and color, defining a shape on a Three-Dimensional ornament, or softening the mounds of snow on a greeting card. Glitter comes in many colors and styles, so there are plenty of options to choose from. Consider the particular project you are working on, and let your imagination be your guide.

You can attach glitter to paper castings with Craft or White Glue, a Glue Pen or Spray Adhesive.

If you want to apply glitter to a limited, defined area, a Glue Pen, or White Glue thinned with a little water and applied with a brush both work well. Spread the glue on the area you want to decorate, then sprinkle on some glitter while the glue is still wet. Allow the glue to dry for a few minutes, then tap the edge of the casting over a sheet of paper. The paper will catch the excess glitter, so you can save it for another project.

If you are applying glitter to a broad area, you can use White Glue or Spray Adhesive. Paint the area to be decorated with thinned White Glue, using a larger brush, and proceed as described above. If you are using Spray Adhesive, spread a large piece of newspaper over your work surface. Place your paper casting in the middle. Spray the project lightly, holding the can at a distance of about 12". A large area of the casting will be covered with a film of adhesive, so be very careful to sprinkle glitter just on the areas where you want it. Spray Adhesive is particularly useful for decorating the background of a card *before* you attach a cast paper image to it. For example, if you want to make a Christmas card of a reindeer flying through a starry sky, place your blank card on the newspaper, spray it lightly, and sprinkle with shiny stars. When the glue is dry,

attach your painted reindeer paper casting with Hot Glue. Then, if you want, apply a little glitter powder with thinned White Glue to the antlers and saddle blanket.

An easy way to apply glitter powder is to mix equal quantities of White Glue and water in a saucer or custard cup and add the powder directly to it. You can then literally paint on the glitter.

Please note: If you use Spray Adhesive, do so in a well ventilated area, and follow all precautions on the can. We do not recommend the use of this product by children.

Spray Adhesive applied over powdered metallic watercolors will dull their shine.

Be sure to wash your brush well in warm, soapy water after using it with glue.

Ribbons

There are hundreds of beautiful ribbons now available with which you can decorate handcast paper projects. In addition to satin ribbons, there are grossgrain and moire ribbons, ones with gold edging, ones made from the sheerest organdy, printed and patterned ribbons, gold, silver and copper ribbons, ribbons with wire edging so that they will hold intricate shapes, and more. Your local craft or fabric store should stock a dazzling array.

Ribbons should be attached to cast paper projects with Hot Glue. It is quick and easy, and it holds well. (Just be careful not to burn yourself. Hot Glue really is *hot*.)

You can glue bows on Valentine cards or simple loops on handcast ornaments. If you would like to make a loop with a bow on top for one of your ornaments, tie a narrow, 18" piece of ribbon around a cardboard tube 1-1/2" in diameter. Make a firm square knot. Tie a bow on top of the knot. Slide the ribbon off the end of the tube. You now have a loop with a bow on top. Hot Glue the loop to the back of your ornament, and trim the tails decoratively in a V shape or on the diagonal.

You can make a ribbon banner with writing on it for a special greeting card. (See the Valentine on page 50) First, cut a piece of 1/2" wide satin ribbon of the proper length for your project. Paint the back of it with a liberal coat of rubber cement, and stick the ribbon down on a piece of plain, white typing paper. Let the rubber cement dry. Using a fine tip gold marker, write your message on the ribbon. When the ink is dry, peel up the ribbon, and stick it to your card with a little more rubber cement. It makes a very dramatic accent.

Pressed Dried Flowers

Make beautiful Valentines or framed art with a nostalgic Victorian feeling, by gluing dried pressed flowers and leaves around a handcast paper image. Simply mix equal parts of White Glue and water in a saucer or custard cup, and paint the mixture on the back of a dried flower. Gently position the flower on the card, and press firmly.

If you cannot find pressed flowers in a hobby store, it is easy to make your own.

Collect a bunch of flowers, ferns and greens on a dry day. Choose small, flat flowers, not fat ones, such as roses or Shasta daisies. Place the flowers on blotting paper, in an old telephone directory, or on a sheet of newspaper, spacing them so they don't touch. Cover with another sheet of newspaper. Place a heavy book on top. After a few days, check and see if your flowers are dry. If they aren't, give them a few more days.

Some of our favorite flowers for pressing are pansies, columbines, nasturtiums, individual phlox blossoms, alyssum, bridal veil, coral bells, violets and buttercups. Ferns and grey foliaged plants such as dusty miller and artemisia are nice, too.

Scent

The romantic Victorian custom of sending scented letters seems to have been forgotten, but there is no reason not to revive it. Imagine how nice it would be to receive a beautifully decorated handcast Valentine with the fragrance of roses or jasmine.

Add fragrance to your paper by placing a drop of perfume or essential oil on one corner of your artwork. Don't use too much, or it might leave a spot.

THINGS TO
DO WITH
HANDCAST
PAPER IMAGES

Ornaments and Decorations

You can make all kinds of wonderful hand-cast paper ornaments using Brown Bag Paper Art and Brown Bag Cookie Art ceramic molds. Ornaments needn't be confined to Christmas. You can decorate with handcast paper all year around. Deck your front door with Ghosts or Jack-O-Lanterns for Halloween, hang hearts from your mantle on Valentine's Day, enliven the front of your refrigerator with a Gourmet Kitty or a group of Big Fat Pigs, put a painted Birthday Bear Ornament on your child's door on that special day, cover your Christmas tree with Musical Angels, Stars and gilded Acorns and Pears. The ideas just keep coming.

Here is a selection of special ornaments, along with instructions on how you can make them, too. Let these projects spark your imagination.

Lacey Heart Ornament

Cut 2" bands from around the perimeter of two 10" paper doilies. Place a small dab of Hot Glue at the center top of any handcast paper heart, and attach one end of one of the doily strips. Now, run a bead of Hot Glue about 2" along the top edge of the heart. Gather the doily strip slightly and press it against the Hot Glue.

Proceed around the heart, working in 2" sections, until you reach the bottom point. Trim. Repeat on the other half of the heart, again starting at the middle of the top. Decorate with dried or silk flowers, a bow, and a ribbon loop, all affixed with Hot Glue.

Refrigerator Art

Handcast three Big Fat Pigs. Paint them a delicate pink, adding darker pink to highlight the cheeks and the fat, round rear end. Paint the bows different colors. Hot Glue 1" round magnets (available at craft stores) onto the center of the backs of the paper castings. Stick the Pigs to your refrigerator door.

An Autumn Swag For Your Door

Cast 7 or 8 Acorn Ornament halves, and paint them gold. Trim off the deckled edges with scissors. Cut 3 or 4 well branched twigs, strip them of leaves, and bind them tightly together 4" from the top, using thin wire. This will form your frame. Using Hot Glue, attach artificial autumn leaves, available in sprays from craft stores. Cover the twigs well. Glue on the golden Acorn halves. Tie a big bow around the twigs, covering the wire binding. Attach a wire loop for hanging.

Star Spangled Banner

Cut long, curved strips of red, white and blue cloth. Sew them together edge to edge, with the red strip on top, followed by the white, then the blue. Make a narrow hem along both margins of your banner.

Cast a number of paper Stars. Paint them gold. Hot Glue a sturdy plastic garbage bag fastener vertically to the back of one of the points of each Star. Clasp the plastic fastener around the banner, positioning a Star every 18". Use string to tie your Star Spangled Banner to a railing or banister. Insert small flags through the fasteners' loops so that they protrude from behind the Stars, if you like.

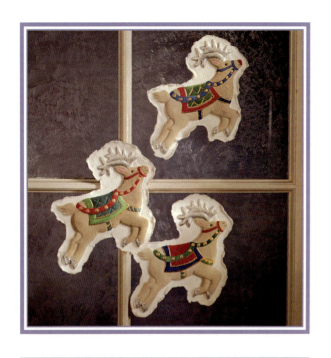

Reindeer Window Decorations

Paint handcast paper Prancer reindeer, using tempera or watercolors. When they are dry, press a piece of moldable plastic adhesive to the back of the reindeer, behind the antlers. Press the paper casting with adhesive firmly against the inside of a window. If you prefer, you can attach a herd of reindeer across a wall, using the same technique. This is a great project for elementary schools.

Musical Angels

Cast a number of Brown Bag Paper Art Musical Angels. Paint and decorate them as you choose, then carefully cut them out. Cut down along the sides of the elbows and along the side of the lute, if your Angel is holding a lute. Bend the skirt into a cone, and Hot Glue the edges together. If you want your Angel Ornaments to truly appear to float, you can Hot Glue them to branches of your Christmas tree. Otherwise, attach narrow ribbon loops to the backs of the Angels' heads, so you can hang them.

Centerpiece - Bowl of Iridescent Pears

Cast as many Pear Ornaments as it will take to fill a pretty glass bowl. Paint the stems of the Pears brown and the leaves green. Paint one half Pear with a thick coat of Liquitex™ Iridescent Gold acrylic paint. While the paint is still wet, mix a little red acrylic paint with a little gold, and paint a rosy blush on the side of the Pear. Blend the color. Paint the rest of the Pears in a similar manner. When dry, glue Pear halves together, decorate with a little glitter if you like, and arrange them in the bowl.

Wreath Ornaments

Handcast two Holly Wreaths for each finished ornament. Use red acrylic paint to color the holly berries and the bow. Paint the leaves green, varying the shade by mixing a little yellow with the green in some areas, a bit of blue in others. Paint the birds whatever color you choose. When the paint is dry, you can brush on a coat of Acrylic Gloss Medium, if you would like a shiny finish. Hot Glue a ribbon loop with a bow on top (instructions on page 37) on the back of one painted image. Back with another casting using Hot Glue.

47

Special Greeting Cards

ake special, very personal greeting cards by attaching a decorated hand-cast paper image to a card with Hot Glue. You can decorate the card further by gluing on torn pieces of colored paper, glitter, dried flowers, or found objects. Surprise and delight a friend with a special card on a holiday, or any day at all.

To make a greeting card with a handcast image, you can either buy Oversized Cards and Envelopes, or you can make your own.

You will need:

decorated cast paper images
Oversized Greeting Cards or heavy colored paper, available at craft stores
Oversized Envelopes or large white paper for making envelopes
Hot Glue
White Glue or Rubber Cement for sealing the envelopes
Exacto knife
ruler
*cutting mat or piece of cardboard to protect your table**

If you are making your own cards, measure your paper casting and decide how big the card should be. Cut out a piece of the colored paper that is twice that size. Fold it in half and Hot Glue on the paper image. Decorate as you like. If you have chosen a very dark paper, you might want to glue a piece of plain white paper on the right hand inside panel of the card. It will be easier to write legibly on this than on the dark paper.

Now make the envelope. Measure your card carefully. Cut out a piece of paper that looks like the diagram, making panel A 1/2" larger in both directions than your card.

Panel B should be exactly the same size as panel A. Fold in the two side flaps, marked C on the diagram. Fold panel A up over panel B. Glue panel A to the folded-in C flaps. Allow the glue to dry before inserting your greeting card. Fold down flap D, and paste it in place.

Remember, oversized greeting cards require extra postage.

Dritz makes an excellent plastic cutting mat that is marked out in a 1" grid. It makes accurately cutting boxes and envelopes a breeze. They are available at quilting and fabric stores.

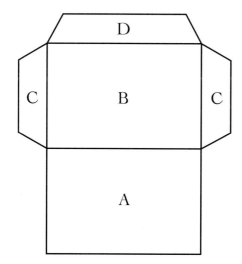

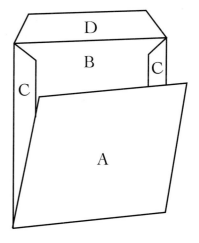

Valentine Card

Paint a handcast Cherub with pale watercolors. Apply glitter powder to the cloud and the tips of the wings. Hot Glue the decorated paper casting to the center of a pink oversized card. Cut a number of small hearts out of red and pink construction paper and rubber cement them around the Cherub. Make a banner with gold writing on it, as described on page 37. Hot Glue the banner in place.

Easter Card

Paint a Juggling Rabbit paper casting with bright colors. Make a 5" X 8" card out of a vividly colored paper. Glue a diagonal strip of another bright paper on top. Hot Glue on the Juggling Rabbit. Squeeze out wiggles of Hot Glue around the rabbit's feet, and while the glue is still warm and soft, press in bunches of cellophane Easter grass. When the glue hardens, trim the grass with scissors.

Graduation Card/
Bon Voyage Card

This card would be appropriate for a graduating student or one leaving for college, for a friend heading off on a trip, or for anyone embarking on a new adventure.

Paint a Flying Pig paper casting with pale pink watercolors or with acrylics. Apply glitter powder to the wings. Tear strips of pastel colored papers, and glue them to your card, overlapping them so that they look like cloud layers. Hot Glue the Flying Pig in place. Decorate the card with more glitter, if you like, and inscribe your message.

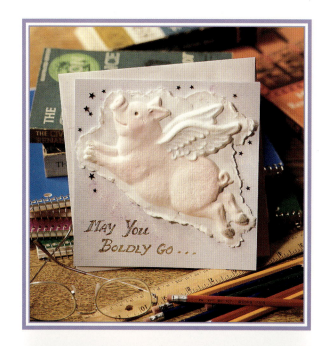

Father's Day

Handcast a Gourmet Kitty and paint it. Paint the frying pan silver, and highlight the fish with silver or gold. Cut out the image. Cut an oval 6" high by 4" wide from a piece of colored paper. Glue it to the center of a 9" X 7" card. With colored pencils, draw around the oval - then again a second time, 1/2" away from the edge. Draw a border around the edge of the card, and Hot Glue the Gourmet Kitty in place. Inscribe your message.

Spring Card

Make a Bunny Garden paper casting. Using thick acrylic paints, color the carrots bright orange. Paint the primroses pale yellow. Next paint the carrot tops and the foliage in a variety of greens. Color the bunny. Now, using thinned, pale acrylics or watercolors, paint the border around the carrots and primroses light blue. The color will bleed only as far as the edges of the painted elements. Paint the bands around the border gold, once the rest of the paint is dry.

Birthday Card

There are all sorts of images you can use to make a very special birthday card; the age and interests of the recipient will have a lot to do with what you choose. We have made a card for a young child, using a Hobby Horse paper casting.

Paint the cast paper image with acrylics or tempera. Use pale colors, mixed with a lot of white, so that the color isn't too bold. When the paper casting is dry, Hot Glue it to a card. Write your message.

Wedding Shower

Make a Two Swans paper casting. Paint the water lilies and bull rushes with fairly thick acrylic paint. When it is dry, color the sky, water and borders with delicate washes of either acrylic or watercolors. The thin paint will not bleed onto the area that was previously painted with thick acrylics. Paint the stars and the waves in the border silver, and the bands around the border gold. Glue two glitter hearts to the tips of the swans' beaks. Hot Glue the decorated image to a pink card.

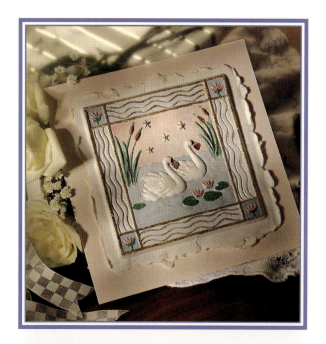

Autumn Friendship Card

Paint a Mr. Squirrel paper casting with tempera, Brown Bag Paper Art Watercolors, or acrylics. While the image is drying, cut out a number of 1-1/2" to 2" paper leaves from colored construction paper. Use Hot Glue to attach Mr. Squirrel and the leaves to a card. Inside the card, draw or paint a picture of an acorn, and write your inscription, "I'm Nuts About You!"

Snowman

This is a very easy project for children. Use either tempera or Brown Bag Paper Art Watercolors to paint a handcast Snowman. When dry, position him on a 5-1/2" X 8" card, and lightly mark his location with a pencil. Paint an area for the Snowman to sit with White Glue thinned with an equal amount of water. Apply glitter to look like snow banks. Hot Glue the Snowman in place. (An adult should help with the Hot Glue.)

St. Nicholas

Make a St. Nicholas paper casting, and paint it with acrylics. Use bright, intense colors, and keep your paint fairly thick. When dry, Hot Glue St. Nicholas on a 5-1/2" X 8" card. Either a bright Christmas green or cobalt blue will complement the red robes. Apply a galaxy of stars around St. Nick's head. Glue a sheet of white paper on the inside right hand panel of the card, since it is hard to write legibly on so dark a paper.

Child's Stocking

Make a handcast Child's Stocking. Paint it with acrylics, using bright, Holiday colors. Paint the jingle bells silver, and highlight the stocking and toys with gold. Hot Glue the decorated image to a dark green 6" X 7" card. Attach an assortment of glitter stars to the background, using a brush and thinned White Glue. Glue a sheet of white paper on the inside right hand panel of the card, since it is hard to write legibly on so dark a paper.

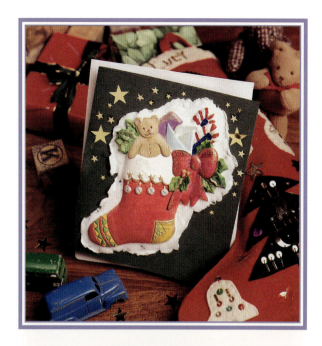

Dove of Peace

Cast a paper Dove. Paint the beak, eye and olive branch gold. Cut a curved "stem" and a number of pointy leaves from olive green construction paper. Crease the leaves in half. Lay the stem diagonally across a pale blue 7" X 7" card, and glue it in place. Hot Glue the Dove in the middle of the card. Glue the leaves around the Dove along the stem, sticking down only the half of the leaf nearest the stem. This way, the other half will stick out a bit.

Cast Paper Gift Tags

Nice looking gift tags are very hard to find, and if you do manage to locate some, they are usually sold singly, and at a high price. It makes good sense to make your own.

It is easy to cast tiny paper images and Hot Glue them to little cards. The relief from the casting is nice enough that you don't have to decorate the tags further, but it's always fun to, anyway.

Angel Gift Tags

Angel gift tags can be very elegant with minimal painting. If you are making quite a few, it is a good idea to mix up skin colored paint and paint all the faces and hands first. Acrylics and tempera work best for this. When the faces are dry, paint the features, and a pale flush on the cheeks. Paint the hair. Lastly, paint the halos, musical instruments, stars and border lines gold. Of course, if you would like to apply a little iridescent glitter powder to the wings, that would be pretty, but the tags look beautiful without it, too.

Flower and Berry Tags

Mix up a batch of paper pulp, and pour 2 cups into a sieve to drain briefly. Pour the pulp into a Flowers & Berries Shortbread Pan. Sop out water with a sponge, then press firmly with kitchen towels. Dry. Remove the paper from the pan, trim the edges with scissors, and cut apart segments. Paint and decorate images as you choose. Hot Glue them to tags. These would also make great labels for jam and jelly jars. *(see page 70 for detailed instructions for casting paper in shortbread pans)*

Framed Art

The objects on the walls of a house tell a lot about the people who live there. You can make truly unique framed art to fill your walls or to give as gifts.

You will need:

paper casting that you want to frame
ruler
mat board for mounting your paper casting
frame and glass to fit

foam core board (available at art supply stores)
cardboard backing
Exacto knife, or other sharp hobby knife
Hot Glue
glazing points (available at hardware stores)
brown kraft paper
White Glue
sponge
small screw eyes (available at hardware stores)
picture hanging wire (available at hardware stores)

1. Mount a decorated paper casting on a sturdy mat board. There is a wide variety of mat board colors available. Cut a cardboard backing board exactly the same size. Measure the outside dimensions carefully and either make or purchase a frame of the proper size.

2. Choose a deep frame that will accommodate the thickness of the paper casting. Most frames are made on the assumption that the object to be framed is flat. This is not the case with handcast paper images made from Brown Bag Cookie Art or Brown Bag Paper Art molds. In fact, part of their charm is their dimensionality.

3. To accommodate the thickness of the handcast image being framed, you will have to make "spacers" to hold the glass away from the surface of your art.

To make a spacer, measure the heighth of your image from the mat board. With an Exacto knife, cut 4 strips of foam-core board, just a little wider than the heighth of the paper image. Cut the strips so that they fit the perimeter of the mat board. You may want to paint your spacers to match the color of your mat board using acrylic paint.

4. Run a thin bead of Hot Glue along one edge of the mat board. Place one of the foam-core strips, cut edge down, on the glue, and hold it in place until the glue sets. Continue gluing the strips in place. You now have something that looks like a shallow tray with a decorated handcast paper image in it.

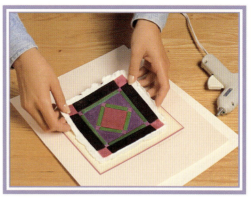

1

3

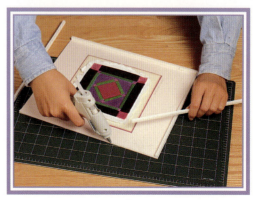

4

5

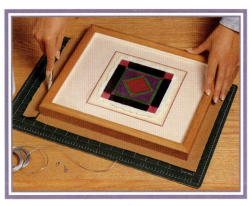

6

5. Turn the frame over on a work surface so the open back is facing up. Clean the glass and set it in the frame, being careful not to get fingerprints on it. Invert the mat board with your image on it, and place it over the glass. Cover the back of the mat board with the piece of cardboard. Push the glazing points into the inside back of the frame at 3" intervals so they hold everything snugly in place.

Your paper art is now framed. To finish the job and make it look really professional, you will want to cover the back with taut brown paper and attach screw eyes and picture wire for hanging.

6. Cut a piece of brown kraft paper a bit bigger than the back of your work. Run a generous bead of white glue along the back of the frame. Spread the glue to a thin, even layer with your finger. The glue should cover, but shouldn't drip over the edges of the frame. Place the kraft paper on top of the frame. Gently press it in place, then let it dry.

When the glue is completely dry, run the Exacto knife around the outside of the frame and cut off the overhanging paper. Now wet your sponge and wring it out so that it is just damp. Sponge the back of the paper, using long, sweeping strokes. Try not to get the very edges damp, as this might loosen the glue.

As the paper dries, it will shrink and become taut. Twist the screw eyes into the back of the frame, add the picture wire, and proudly hang your finished work of art.

Please note: If you want to make a deep, shadow box frame for one half of a 3-dimensional ornament or for a nostalgic heart surrounded by dried flowers, the procedure is exactly the same as described on pages 58-60. You will just have to be sure that your foam core spacer is large enough to accommodate the depth of the image.

Paper Baskets

*I*t is fun to make pretty paper baskets. You can fill them with fresh flowers for May Day, special rocks or shells that you have picked up on a trip to the beach, potpourri or dried flowers.

You will need:
handmade sheets of wet paper
(see section on Making Sheets of Paper,
page 12)
small basket to use as a form
sponge
towels
three 12" pieces of flexible wire
Hot Glue
raffia   (available at craft stores)

2

3

1. Choose a small basket to use as a form. When using a colored basket, test the color fastness before proceeding. To do so, place a small piece of wet paper on the bottom of the basket and blot it with a sponge. After an hour, peel it off. If the color bleeds onto the paper, don't use the basket, unless of course, you like the effect.

2. Drape the inside of the basket with overlapping strips of wet paper. You may want to apply unevenly torn pieces that are of different colors.

3. When the surface of the basket is covered, sponge off the excess water with a sponge. Blot with a towel, pressing gently

so that you pick up the detail of the basket's weave. Set the basket aside to air dry.

4. Wrap the three wires with raffia. Braid them together loosely, and bend them in an arc.

4

5. When the paper is completely dry, take it off the basket form. To do this, wiggle both the paper and the basket. The paper should come away easily. Trim the top edge.

6. Trim the ends of the handle to the length you want, using a pair of wire cutters. Be sure you leave 1-1/2" of extra handle on both ends so you can attach it to the inside of your basket. Position the handle, and Hot Glue it in place on the inside of the basket.

6

7. Decorate your basket with paint, ribbons, dried flowers, or whatever you like.

Handmade Boxes

Boxes can be as wonderful as whatever it is they contain. I know that I have bought things because I loved the packages they came in. I still have the boxes, long after the contents are gone. These boxes are themselves art.

Here are some ideas and patterns for making special boxes. Start here, and *play!*

SIMPLE SQUARE TWO PIECE BOX

This box has a separate lid that slides down over the bottom part of the box. These instructions make a box that is 3-1/2" square by 2-3/8" high. If you would like to make a box that is a different size, follow the instructions in principle, but change the proportions. Just remember to make the bottom of the box about 1/8" smaller than the top, so that the top can slide down over it.

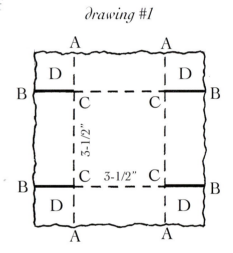

drawing #1

You will need:
Sheet of handmade paper, about 6-1/2" square
8" X 8" sheet of very heavy colored paper or Bristol Board
  (from an art supply store)
Exacto knife or pair of scissors
rubber cement
ruler
*cutting mat or piece of cardboard to protect your table**

You can use plain, colored or laminated paper for your box to create special effects. First, make the top of the box.

1. With a pencil, lightly mark out a 3-1/2" square in the middle of your handmade paper, extending all lines to the edge. See drawing #1.

2. With a sharp Exacto knife or pair of scissors, make 4 cuts from B to C.

3. Crease the paper along lines A and B. Fold the two short side panels up so they are perpendicular to the bottom. (See drawing #2).

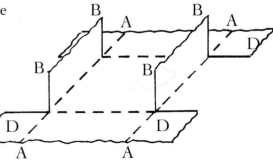

drawing #2

4. Fold up the long box sides, lapping the D panels over the short box sides and each other to form the lid. Glue the sides of the box in place with rubber cement. The box top will have an attractive ragged edge.

Follow the same procedure to make the bottom of the box, but with these differences:

1. The size will be different. Cut an 8" square of very heavy paper or Bristol Board. Measure 2-5/16" in from the edge and draw a light pencil line. Do this on all four sides of the paper. See drawing #4.

2. Construct the box bottom as described above, but lap the small square D panels inside rather than outside the box. This will give a smooth, finished look to the work.

drawing #3

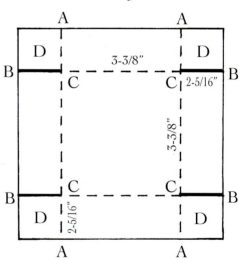

drawing #4

Dritz makes an excellent plastic cutting mat that is marked out in a 1" grid. It makes cutting boxes and envelopes accurately a breeze. They are available at quilting and fabric stores.

ONE PIECE
FOLD UP BOX

This pattern makes a 2-1/2" square box that is 1-3/4" deep. You can enlarge the box, keeping the same proportions, by putting the pattern on a Xerox machine that enlarges and reduces.

You Will Need:
heavy colored paper or Bristol Board
* (available at art stores)*
rubber cement
Exacto knife, or other sharp craft knife
ruler
Hot Glue
small, decorated cast paper image
a cutting mat, marked off in inches, is very
* helpful, but not essential.*
* If you don't have one,*
* you will need a*
* piece of cardboard to*
* use as a cutting mat.*

Following the pattern below, cut out a box of Bristol Board or heavy colored paper. All the solid lines in the pattern indicate cutting lines; all the dotted lines are fold lines.

Fold the box into a square, and using rubber cement, glue panel C to the inside of panel B2. Fold both panel D's toward each other. Fold panel E1 over the D panels, then fold E2 over E1, and glue it in place, using rubber cement.

This will form the body of the box.

Fold both F panels toward each other. Fold panel G down and tuck panel H in to close your box.

You can now Hot Glue a decorated small cast paper image to the top of the box as the finishing touch.

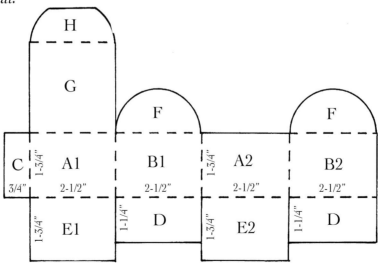

DECORATED ONE PIECE FOLD UP BOX WITH A VAULTED LID

You can enlarge this box by putting the pattern on a Xerox Machine that enlarges and reduces.

You will need:

heavy colored paper or Bristol Board
  (available at art stores)
rubber cement
Exacto knife, or other sharp knife
ruler
Hot Glue
small, decorated cast paper image
2' piece of 1/4" satin ribbon
a cutting mat, marked off in inches, is very helpful,
  but not essential. If you don't have one,
  you will need a piece of cardboard to use as
  a cutting mat.

Following the pattern below, cut out a box of Bristol Board or heavy colored paper. All the solid lines in the pattern indicate cutting lines; all the dotted lines indicate fold lines. Crease the box on all dotted lines.

1. Crease the fold lines, then fold the body of the box together. Using rubber cement, glue panel C to the inside of panel B2. Fold both of the D panels toward each other. Fold panel E1 over the D panels, then fold E2 over that, and glue it in place. The body of the box is now put together.

2. Fold over panel F. Now bend panel G over, and tuck the tab into the slit between panels F and A2. You are now ready to decorate your vaulted box.

3. With the box lying on its back, lay the ribbon vertically across the front. 8" should extend above the top edge of panel A2. Being careful to center your decorated cast paper image, Hot Glue it over the ribbon and onto the front panel of the box. Wrap the longer portion of the ribbon around the back of the box and over the top. Tie a bow above the cast paper image. This will hold the lid of the box in place and will be very pretty.

You can fill your decorated vaulted box with any number of small gifts, but the box itself may be the best gift of all.

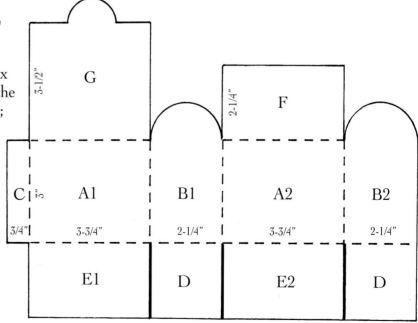

Shell Boxes

Hinged, delicate paper shells tied with satin ribbons make one of the prettiest, most unusual boxes anywhere. You can paint them with pale washes of color and dust them with glitter powder. What a wonderful package for potpourri, fruit candies, or maybe even a pearl necklace.

2

3

You Will Need:

paper pulp
sieve
sponge
kitchen towels
large, open shells (scallop shells work well. They can be purchased in many gourmet cook stores where they are sold as individual dishes for seafood. You can collect some nice shells on a trip to the beach.)
small bowl
small, sharp scissors
Hot Glue
15" of 3/8" satin ribbon
3" section of 3/8" satin ribbon

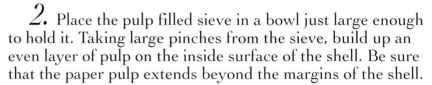

1. Make a batch of paper pulp as directed. Pour about 3/4 to 1 cup of pulp into a sieve to drain until the water stops running and just drips.

2. Place the pulp filled sieve in a bowl just large enough to hold it. Taking large pinches from the sieve, build up an even layer of pulp on the inside surface of the shell. Be sure that the paper pulp extends beyond the margins of the shell.

3. While holding the paper pulp covered shell in one hand, gently press the pulp with a sponge to absorb water. Repeat. Firmly press with a folded kitchen towel to absorb even more water and force the paper fibers up against the shell so they pick up all the detail. Allow the paper to dry completely. Do not dry shells in a microwave.

4. When the paper is dry, carefully remove it from the shell. Trim the edges with a small, sharp pair of scissors, making sure that the back hinge edge of the shell is cut straight and clean. Make a second paper shell. You will need to have two paper shells to make a Shell Box.

4

5. Paint or decorate the paper shells, if you like.

6. Cut a 3" long piece of ribbon. With the inside of one paper shell facing up, run a tiny bead of Hot Glue along the straight back hinge edge. Press one margin of the ribbon against the glue, and let it set.

6

7. Turn the shell over, so that the ribbon is sticking out from under the back rim of the shell. Run a tiny bead of hot glue along the protruding margin of the ribbon. Press the other shell hinge on to the glue, making sure to leave a narrow gap between the two paper shells. You now have a pair of paper shells with a ribbon hinge holding them together. Trim off the extra ribbon.

8. Cut the 15" piece of ribbon in half. Place a tiny button of Hot Glue on the middle of the inside front edge of one shell. Press one end of a ribbon onto it. Repeat on the other side. These two ribbons can be tied in a bow to fasten your Shell Box closed.

7

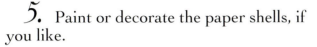

Flower Cones

There is a charming old tradition of going around to neighbors' houses early in the morning on May Day, leaving a tiny basket of fresh spring flowers hung on the door knob. These elegant little cone shaped baskets are perfect for this.

You don't have to use these Cones just for flowers, however; they make wonderful baskets for hard candies, potpourri, or dried flowers as well.

You will need:
a batch of paper pulp
Brown Bag Cookie Art ceramic
shortbread pan - Wildflower, Hearts and Flowers, or Thistle design
sieve
sponge
kitchen towel
Hot Glue
30" satin ribbon, 1/4" wide
scissors
lace
paints
glitter and White glue

1. Make up a batch of paper pulp as directed on page 7. Pour about 2 cups of pulp into a sieve to drain for about thirty seconds.

2. Pour the pulp into a round or octagonal Brown Bag Cookie Art ceramic shortbread pan. Pat it out with your finger tips so that it evenly covers the bottom of the pan. Be sure the edges are nice and even.

3. Sop out as much water as you can, pressing on the pulp with your sponge. Take a folded kitchen towel, and press the pulp into the mold. This will absorb still more water and will assure that the paper picks up all of the detail.

4. Allow the paper to dry in the pan. Leave the pan on the counter overnight, or put it in the oven set at 150° for about four hours. Do not use a microwave.

5. When the paper is completely dry, carefully peel it out of the shortbread pan. You might need to loosen one edge with the point of a sharp knife to get it started.

6. Trim the edges of the paper casting, then cut it in half. Paint and decorate as you like.

7. Crease the paper casting along the score lines and fold it together to form a cone. Run a bead of Hot Glue down one edge and glue the cone together.

2

3

5

8. If you want to trim the top of your cone with lace, now is the time. You can use real lace or paper lace trimmed from the edge of a doily. Starting with the seam where the cone was glued together, place a line of hot glue along the inside top edge of one section. Press lace into the glue, being careful not to burn your fingers. Continue gluing on the lace neatly until you reach the place where you started.

9. Glue on the ribbon. The ribbon serves two functions; first, it hides the seam where you glued the cone together, and second, it forms a decorative handle.

Fold the ribbon in half. Place a dot of hot glue on the tip of the cone and attach the mid-point of the ribbon to it. Now run a line of hot glue up the seam where the cone was joined together, and press the ribbon over it. Glue the other half of the ribbon on the opposite side of the cone.

Firmly tie the two ribbons together with a square knot to form a looped handle over the cone. Tie a bow on top of the square knot.

If you have Hot Glued the seam of the cone neatly, you can simply place a dab of glue inside two opposite corners of the top edge of the cone and attach two shorter sections of ribbon. Tie as above. Your cone is now ready to be filled with whatever goodies you want.

7

8

9

Acorn Place Card Holders

Not often, but every once in a while, we give a big dinner party. It may be a family reunion, a Christmas feast, or an engagement or wedding supper. With lots of people at the table, place cards are a real help with traffic control.

You can write guests' names on plain white cards and arrange them at each place setting, or you can add an additional festive touch by making gilded Acorn Place Card Holders.

You will Need:
*Brown Bag Paper Art Three
  Dimensional Acorn mold
paper pulp (see page 7)
supplies for casting 3-d paper (page 10)
gold paint
medium brush
Hot Glue
plain cards, 3-1/2" by 2-1/4"*

Cast as many paper Acorn Ornaments as the number of expected guests. (See pages 10 and

11 for detailed instructions.) Remember that each complete Acorn will require both a front and back half. Make sure that the ragged, deckle edge extending around the margin of your Acorn is neat and even. If they aren't, you can trim them when they are dry with "Deckle Scissors", available through some hobby stores.

When your paper castings are dry, paint the Acorns gold. If you are using the powdered watercolor metallic paints, be sure to mix them with Acrylic Gloss Medium, so that the gold won't rub off with handling.

Run a bead of Hot Glue on the back of one half Acorn, only putting glue behind the bottom, nut part, and *half* of the cap. Quickly press another Acorn casting against the Hot Glue. Repeat the process with all of the Acorns.

Write the names of your guests on the cards. Slide a card between the unglued area of the two halves of the Acorn caps. Place the card and gilded Acorn holder beside each plate.

Decorate A Gift Box

You can Hot Glue a decorated paper casting to the top of a gift box to make a truly spectacular present. Here are a couple of ideas.

BIRTHDAY BOX

1. Wrap your present with plain, colored paper.

2. Make a Birthday Bear paper casting and paint it with whatever medium you choose. When the paint is dry, poke a small hole right above the Bear's right paw.

3. Cut five "balloons" out of colored construction paper. Tie a thin, white piece of string around the mouth of each balloon.

4. Glue one of the tails of the string to the back of the balloon and trim it short; leave the other long string end hanging.

5. Set the Bear in position on the box. Place a dab of Hot Glue behind the pompom on his hat, and stick him down. Set the balloons in place, and Hot Glue them down as well.

6. Now, carefully poke the long string ends from the balloons through the hole above the Bear's paw, and pull them taut.

7. Finish Hot Gluing the Birthday Bear casting in place. You can further decorate the top of your package with swirls of glitter and stars. Use diluted White Glue and brush to apply the glitter.

WEDDING BOX

You Will Need:

cast paper heart
band of lace long enough to go around your box
lace edged doily
1-1/2" wide gold, wire edged ribbon
dried roses
Hot Glue

1. Wrap your package with pale, plain paper. Hot Glue the band of lace around the sides of the box, being careful to make the cut ends neat. You might want to start and end on a corner, depending on the particular lace pattern.

2. Set the lace edged doily on top of the box. Carefully Hot Glue it in place. Next, glue on the cast paper heart.

3. Tie a big bow from the wire edged gold ribbon. Pull the knot tight and puff up the loops. Hot Glue the bow above the center of the heart. Arrange the tails decoratively and fix them in place with a tiny button of glue.

4. Finally, trim the stems of the dried roses and glue them in place.

Appendix

MAKING A MOLD FOR SHEETS OF PAPER

If you would like to make sheets of hand made paper, you will need to use a "paper mold", consisting of a frame covered with screening, and a "deckle", or empty frame of the same size. Here are simple directions for making your own.

You will need:

eight 8" stretcher rails (available at art supply stores)
  (These make the frames over which a painter stretches his canvas)
tube of silicone caulking
two 12" squares of nylon window screening
2 large rubber bands

Stretcher rails come with tabs and slots cut into the corners so that you can assemble them by simply pushing them together. Assemble 2 squares. One of these empty frames will serve as your deckle.

Lay the other frame on a work surface. Run a generous bead of silicone caulking around the inside perimeter of the opening, 1" back from the edge. Place one of the pieces of nylon screening on top and press gently. Be sure that the screening is nice and flat. Allow the caulking to dry completely.

You will use the 2 rubber bands and the other piece of screening in the paper making process. See page 12 for complete instructions.

MAKING ROUND OR OVAL SHEET PAPER MOLDS

You can change the shape of your paper-making frame to produce sheets of paper that suit a particular project. For example, a round or oval sheet of hand made paper is a lovely backing for a cast heart image.

To make a round or oval paper making frame, you will need:

nylon window screening
tube of silicone caulking (available at hardware stores)
a two-part embroidery hoop (available at craft and fabric stores)

1. Run a bead of silicone caulking around the top edge of the smaller, inside hoop.

Draw your screening material taut, and stick it on to the hoop. Allow silicone to dry completely. Trim away excess screen.

2. This smaller, screen covered hoop will serve as your paper making frame. Slide the larger, outer hoop down just over the edge of the smaller frame. It will act as the deckle. You will not need rubber bands to hold the two together.

3. Hold the mold, deckle side up, just beneath the surface of the water in the plastic tub as you pour in paper pulp. Pat the pulp with your finger tips to even it, and proceed as described on page 12.

MAKING UNUSUAL SHAPED PAPER SHEET MOLDS

You don't have to be limited to simple rectangles, squares, circles and ovals. If you would like to make an unusual shaped piece of paper, you can do that, too. Say you want to make a star.

In addition to your regular square or rectangular sheet papermaking mold you will need:
*1/4" thick piece of foam-core board, available at art
   supply stores
an Exacto knife, or other small, sharp hobby knife
either varnish or hide glue
1" wide paint brush*

1. Cut out a piece of foam-core that is the same size as your paper frame. Place the deckle on the foam-core, and using a pencil, lightly draw around the inside of the wooden frame. Remove the deckle.

2. Draw the shape of the star on the foam-core, being sure that you leave at least a 1/4" margin between the outside of the star and the line that shows the inside edge of the deckle. Using the Exacto knife, carefully cut out the star and discard it. You now have a star stencil.

3. Seal your foam-core stencil with two coats of hide glue or varnish, allowing the sealant to dry between coats.

4. When the stencil is completely dry, place it on top of the paper frame. Place the deckle on top of the stencil, and put rubber bands around the mold to hold everything together. Float the mold in the tub of water.

5. Pour about 1 to 1-1/2 cups of paper pulp into the floating mold. Pat the pulp lightly with your finger tips to spread it evenly in the star.

6. Holding the frame level, lift it out of the tub, and let the water drain for about 20 seconds. Tip the mold, and let it drain for another 10 seconds.

7. Remove the rubber bands and lift off the deckle. Carefully lift off the stencil. Place the piece of nylon screening over the newly formed sheet of paper, and press it gently with the sponge.
Proceed as described in the section on Making Sheets of Paper.

Sources

Throughout this book, we refer to a number of products. Many, such as nylon screening, Hot Glue, Exacto craft knives, and acrylic paints, are readily available in hardware, craft, hobby, and art supply stores. Some supplies are a little harder to find.

Here is a list of some of the supplies we mention, along with places to find them.

Gold and Silver Paints

Acrylic: Jo Sonja® Rich Gold is dark, brassy, and opaque. This paint covers beautifully and flows well. It mixes poorly with other acrylic paints, and not at all with watercolors. If you would like to have a softer, less brassy gold, use Jo Sonja Pale Gold. Available through many craft and hobby stores, and through a number of art supply stores. Jo Sonja Silver is grey and not very shiny.

Acrylic: Liquitex® Iridescent Gold is pale, translucent, and delicate. By itself, this paint produces a light yellow, opalescent surface. It mixes beautifully with other acrylic paints to add a warm, iridescent sheen to other colors. Available through art supply stores.

There are also a number of different brands of acrylic metallic paints sold in craft and hobby stores, each with varying properties.

Liquitex® is a registered trademark of Binney & Smith, Inc.

Powdered Metallic Water Colors: Available in 8 different colors. These are easy to use mixed with water, but need to have some acrylic medium mixed in to help bind them permanently to the painting surface. They are beautiful and mix well with all other painting mediums. They can be purchased through mail order from:

Daniel Smith Artist's Materials
4150 First Avenue South
P.O. Box 84268
Seattle, Washington 98124

Daniel Smith has a large catalog and sells a wide variety of artists' supplies. They have an excellent selection of unusual handmade papers, in addition to paints, mediums, stretchers, and brushes.

Metallic Enamels: Top Metallic Gold and Silver - these are made by Pelikan®. They are rich, opaque, and easy to use. They tend to thicken because of

evaporation when you get toward the end of the bottle. Add a little water to thin the enamel, if need be. We find Top Silver to be one of the best, shiniest silvers on the market. Available in art supply stores and some hobby shops, particularly ones that sell model airplanes.

Metallic Inks: Winsor & Newton Gold and Silver inks. These are very similar to metallic enamels. The gold is beautiful and flows well. The silver is less lush, and it tends to look a little more like aluminum than silver. It is acceptable, however. To warm up the Silver Ink so it looks less cold and more silvery, mix in a tiny bit of the gold ink. Available in art supply stores.

Spray Adhesives

There are 3 different spray adhesives readily available in art supply and photography stores. Both Spray Mount™ and Photo Mount™ produce a thin, sticky film. They are excellent for adhering one sheet of paper to another, and for applying glitter to large areas.

Spra-Ment™ is thick and viscous. We much prefer the other two products.

Moldable Plastic Adhesive

There are a number of these on the market. Eberhard Faber® makes a product called Hold It. Moldable adhesives can be purchased in craft stores, as well as in some stationery, art, and hobby stores. We have even found it in the stationery section of dime stores.

Cutting Mats

Dritz makes an excellent plastic cutting mat that is marked out in a 1″ grid. It makes cutting boxes and envelopes accurately a breeze. They are available at quilting and fabric stores.

Brown Bag Cookie Art and Brown Bag Paper Art Molds and supplies are available locally through many craft, gift and gourmet stores, or can be ordered by mail from:

Cookie Art Exchange
P.O. Box 4267
Manchester, New Hampshire 03108

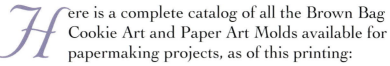

ere is a complete catalog of all the Brown Bag Cookie Art and Paper Art Molds available for papermaking projects, as of this printing:

Quilted Heart
Victorian Heart

Checkered Heart
Bird Folk Heart

Lacey Heart
Hummingbird Heart

Tulip Heart

Swiss Folk Heart
Four Hearts

Cherub
Blossom

Cupid Heart
Rose Heart

Cow Jumping Over the Moon
Sun and Moon

Elaine's Cow
Big Bunny

Juggling Rabbit
Tabby Cat

Wooly Lamb
Big Fat Pig

Cat with Flowers
Contented Cat

Bear Family Album
Mother Goose

Flying Pig
Watermelon Pig

Bunny with Backpack
Easter Egg

Mr. Squirrel
Garden Rabbit

Toy Cow
Toy Lamb

Haunted House
Ghost

Teddy Bear
Happy Birthday Bear

Pennsylvania Heart
Shaker Tree

Skating Bear
Child's Stocking

Beehive
Tulips

Scaredy Cat
Jack-O-Lantern

Wild Strawberries
Little Rabbit

Jingle Cat
Gourmet Kitty

North Pole Cottage
Prancer

Christmas Tree
St. Nicholas

Bedtime Angel
1995 Santa in the Moon

Holly Wreath
Nutcracker

Angel with Lute
Angel with Heart

Gingerbread House
Hobby Horse

Dove
Snowman

Two Swans Greeting Card Kit

Bunny Garden Greeting Card Kit

*Magical Horse
Greeting Card Kit*

*Amish Variable Star Quilt
Greeting Card Kit*

*Schoolhouse Quilt
Greeting Card Kit*

Basket Quilt Greeting Card Kit

*Amish Center Diamond Quilt
Greeting Card Kit*

Reindeer Greeting Card Kit

Angel with Horn Greeting Card Kit

Angel with Lute Ornament Kit
Angel with Trumpet Ornament Kit

Christmas Gift Tag Kit

Celestial Gift Tag Kit

Angel Gift Tag Kit

Cherub Gift Tag Kit

Noel Block
Ornament Kit

Celestial Paper
Casting Mold

Pear Paper
Casting Mold

Acorn Paper
Casting Mold

Star Paper
Casting Mold

Wildflower Shortbread Pan

Hearts and Flowers Shortbread Pan

Cherub Mold with
Handcast Paper Heart Kit

Handcast Paper Art Glitter Kits
Sweethearts, Springtime, Stardust,
Merry Christmas

Bulk Handcast Paper Kit

Oversized Cards and Envelopes
Blues, Pastels, Sweethearts, Vivid Colors,
Clouds, Ivory

Mini Card and Envelope Kits
Mini Pastel Colors, Mini Vivid Colors,
Ivory

Additional Reading

Making Your Own Paper
by Marrianne Saddington
Storey Communications, Inc.
Pownal, Vermont, 1992

Ms. Saddington presents a good, clear introduction to the basics of papermaking in this nice little book. In addition, there are a number of interesting, simple craft projects described.

The Art of Papermaking
by Bernard Toale
Davis Publications, Inc.
Worcester, Massachusetts, 1983

This excellent book covers oriental and European papermaking in great detail. It gives extensive technical information on different fibers, forming, pressing and drying techniques, multiple sheet forming, even building a small paper mill. The section on contemporary sculptural techniques is particularly interesting for those serious about pursuing paper as an art form.

The Art and Craft of Papermaking
by Sophie Dawson
Running Press, Philadelphia, Pennsylvania, 1992

This book covers all the basics of papermaking, as well as papermaking variations, sculptural techniques, and contemporary adaptations. There are lots of easy to follow how-to pictures. The emphasis of the book is on teaching you how to use a variety of papermaking techniques, not on presenting craft projects and ideas.

Paper Pleasures by Faith Shannon
Grove Weidenfeld, in association with Il Papiro
Mitchell Beazley Publishers
New York, New York, 1987

This beautiful book provides an introduction to papermaking, then launches off into an exciting collection of decorating ideas and techniques. The sections on projects made from handmade papers are clear and extensive. The emphasis of the book is on sheet, rather than molded paper.

Notes

Notes

Notes

Notes

Notes